Creative Saxophone Duets

26 stylish duets for beginners

Kellie Santin

Cheryl Clark

OXFORD

UNIVERSITY PRESS

Dear Student,

Creative Saxophone Duets is a fabulous collection of 26 stylish duets that encourage beginner students to enjoy making music with other players both inside and outside of lessons. It is intended to be used alongside *Creative Saxophone* and the duets follow the pace and technical progression of that book. There are also helpful references to the corresponding chapters at the start of each piece.

All of the duets have their own play-along track included on the companion website. The tracks are recorded in two transpositions, one suitable for alto and the other for tenor saxophone and offer the player an authentic experience of performing within an ensemble.

Of course, this book also works on its own and is suitable for any E♭ or B♭ instrument including alto, tenor, soprano, and baritone saxophones, as well as clarinet and trumpet.

Thank you for choosing *Creative Saxophone Duets*. We wish you many hours of happy music making!

Kellie Santin   Cheryl Clark

Contents

Creative
Saxophone
Duets

A tuning note (F♯ for the alto and B for the tenor saxophone)
can be found on the companion website.

Playing along with the tracks

- Visit the Companion Website at **www.oup.com/creativesaxduets** to access and download the play-along tracks.

- The icon on the **left hand side** of the piece title tells you the piece number.

- Tune up using the tuning note located on the companion website. The tuning note is **F#** for the **alto saxophone** and **B♭** for the **tenor saxophone**.

- Both parts are played on the play-along tracks. The top line is found on the left channel, and the bottom line is found on the right channel.

- When you are confident at playing your part, pan left or right (using the balance control on your audio equipment) and mute the part that you are playing. In this way, you can play along with either part as a duet.

- Remember to listen closely to the count-in at the beginning of each tune.

- Count the rests accurately.

- Most importantly, HAVE A GREAT TIME!

Chapters 1–3

1 Let's go

Lively

Kellie Santin

Chapters 1–3

2 Equality of the saxes

Moderately

Kellie Santin

Creative Saxophone Duets

3 Taking it to the limit

Moderately

Cheryl Clark

4 Blast from the past

With spirit

Cheryl Clark

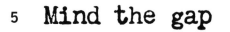

Chapters 1–5

5 Mind the gap

Rock

Kellie Santin

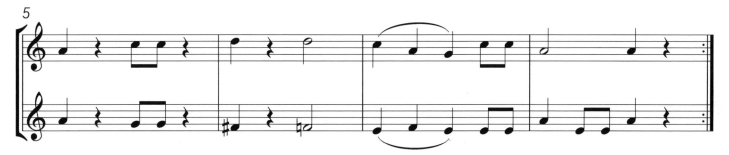

Chapters 1–5

6 Two's company

Waltz

Kellie Santin

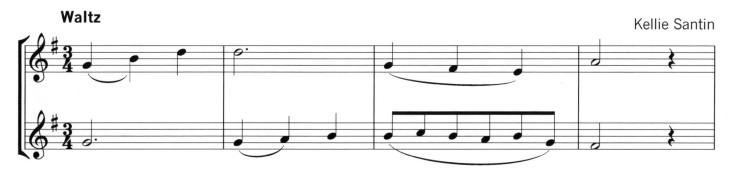

Chapters 1–5

7 Jet lag

Cheryl Clark

Moderately

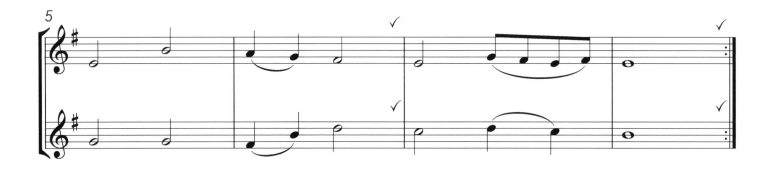

Chapters 1–5

8 Cutting edge

Cheryl Clark

Fast Waltz

Chapters 1–8

9 Craving calypso

Latin

Kellie Santin

10 It's an illusion

Cheryl Clark

Chapters 1–10

11 Elizabeth

Kellie Santin

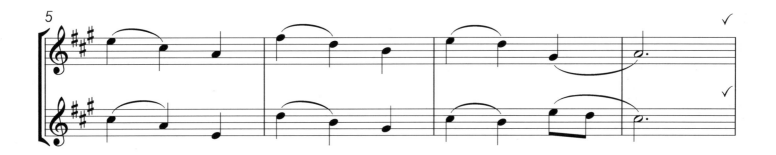

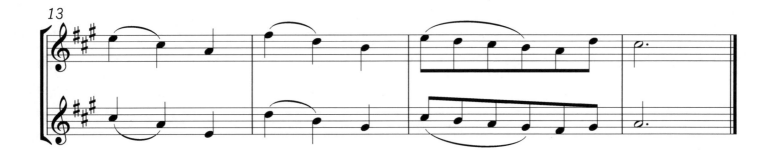

Creative Saxophone Duets

Chapters 1–10

12 Put on your red shoes

Latin

Cheryl Clark

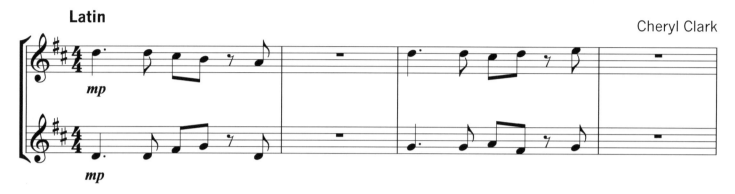

Chapters 1–10

13 The happening thing

Rock

Cheryl Clark

14 Secret agent shuffle

Kellie Santin

Chapters 1–13

15 Anyone for tennis?

Cheryl Clark

Swing

16 In the meantime

Rock

Kellie Santin

Chapters 1–15

17 Empty cupboards

Kellie Santin

Slow Blues

18 Moving right along

Rock

Cheryl Clark

Chapters 1–15

19 Squeaky clean

Swing

Cheryl Clark

20 Never say never

Kellie Santin

Jazz Waltz

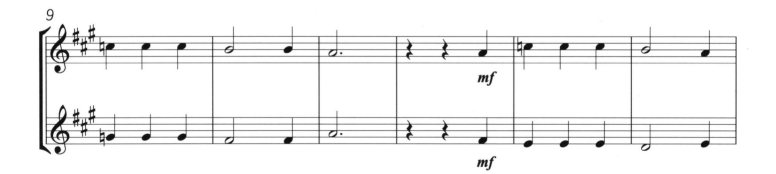

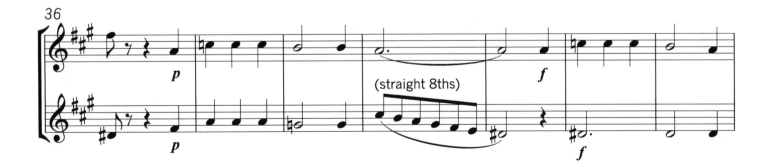

21 Excess baggage

Kellie Santin

Majestically

Swing

22 Cool bananas

Latin

Cheryl Clark

Creative Saxophone Duets

Chapters 1–23

23 Under cover

Kellie Santin

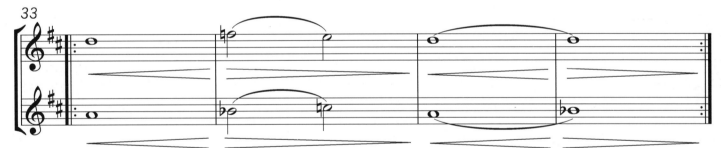

24 Hot off the press

Jazz Waltz

Cheryl Clark

Creative Saxophone Duets

Chapters 1–25

25 Gone troppo

Fast Latin

Cheryl Clark

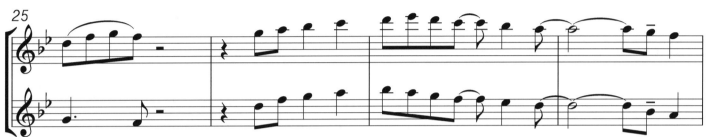

26 And the winner is . . .

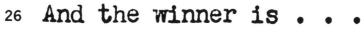

Fast Rock

Kellie Santin